MEN OF GOD

Augustine of Hippo

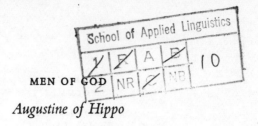

Augustine of Hippo

Mary McCulloch

LONDON
OXFORD UNIVERSITY PRESS
IBADAN NAIROBI ACCRA
1964

Oxford University Press
Amen House, London E.C.4

GLASGOW NEW YORK TORONTO
MELBOURNE WELLINGTON
BOMBAY CALCUTTA MADRAS KARACHI LAHORE DACCA
CAPE TOWN SALISBURY NAIROBI IBADAN ACCRA
KUALA LUMPUR HONG KONG

*The illustrations for this book have been specially drawn
by Taj Ahmed; the map is by Edgar Holloway*

———————

PRINTED IN GREAT BRITAIN BY HEADLEY BROTHERS LTD
109 KINGSWAY LONDON WC2 AND ASHFORD KENT

Contents

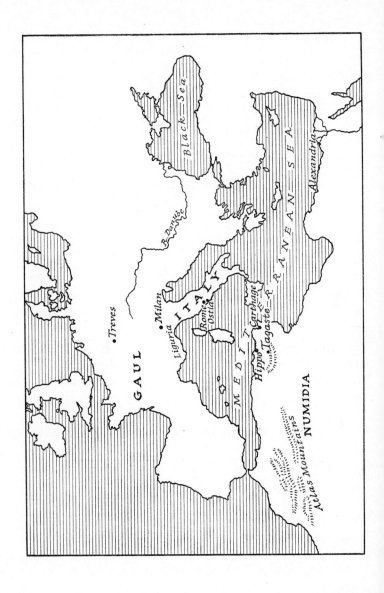

I

The Town of Tagaste

————→••••◆••••←————

ONE day some young boys were playing with a ball outside a little school. They were laughing and shouting as they played together and fought to get the ball from each other. They were all very happy until the time came for them to go back to the classroom. Then their teacher began his lesson: 'One and one make two; two and two make four.' He soon found that several of the boys did not know the lesson that they should have learnt. They had been playing ball instead of doing their school work. The teacher called some of the boys to come to him and he beat them, saying: 'Perhaps this stick will teach you to leave your ball games and to learn your lessons.'

The school was a small school in North Africa, at a place called Tagaste. This little town of Tagaste was about forty miles from the Mediterranean Sea, in that part of Africa which is now known as Algeria. Long ago, that country was called Numidia, a name which meant the land of the wandering tribes.

Numidia lay between the Mediterranean Sea and the huge chain of mountains, the Great Atlas. The lower parts of the land received a good quantity of water from the streams that came down from the mountains; so the fields were green and fertile. The people of Numidia, who lived among the dry, rocky hills were herdsmen, who moved from place to place finding food and water for their herds. Those who lived at Tagaste and at other towns and villages of the plain did not travel about. They had their houses and their fields, where they grew corn and many different kinds of fruit. Much of the corn was sent by sea to Rome, because Numidia was a Province of the Roman Empire.

In the fourth century after the birth of Jesus Christ, the Roman Empire was beginning to fail. When the city of Rome began to build its great empire, the citizens of that empire were free. They could live and work as they chose, if they kept the laws of Rome and did nothing to harm the empire. By the fourth century, however, there had already been wars between the people of the cities and the army.

Most of the soldiers in the army were men who came from country districts, and the time came when they fought against the towns. After these wars, the Emperors of Rome made new laws. They did not allow men to choose where they lived or the work that they did. The new laws were very strict, because the Emperors were afraid that their power might be taken from them.

Besides the quarrels between the citizens and the army, there were quarrels between those who were Christians and those who were not. For a very long time the Roman Emperors attacked the Christians and would not allow them to be free, because the Christians refused to say that the Emperors were gods. But a certain Emperor of Rome, whose name was Constantine, allowed the Christians to be free. In fact, people thought that they would get honour if they were

Christians and many people, who were not really followers of Christ, joined the Christian Church.

In Numidia, there had been a large group of Christians for many years. No one knows exactly how the Christian faith was taken to that country. But it is true that, after Christ had gone back to heaven, the Christian religion began to spread towards the West from Palestine.

There were several reasons for this. First, the teaching given by Christ himself was not for the Jews only but for men and women of all races.

Secondly, Saint Paul and many other Jewish Christians travelled towards Rome and the West, and taught other people as they went.

Thirdly, the Greek language was used in many places along the coast of the Mediterranean Sea, so that Christian teachers did not have to learn new languages in order to teach.

Fourthly, the lands round the Mediterranean Sea were almost all in the Roman Empire. The Romans had built many fine roads, so that it was easy for people to travel from one place to another.

Thus we know that there were many Christians in Tagaste by the middle of the fourth century.

Among the pupils at the little school in Tagaste was a boy named Augustine. Augustine was born on Sunday, 13th November, 354. His father was Patricius,* a native of Tagaste, who owned a few fields but who never became a rich man. Patricius was not a Christian; he was one of the men whom the Romans had appointed to be responsible for the taxes of his district. It was an honour to be one of these men but an honour that few men wanted to have. If the people of the

* Patri'cius

district failed to pay the taxes that were due, then the Romans could take the goods or the money of the responsible men.

So Patricius often had to worry about money and perhaps that is why he was often angry. But Augustine was not always a good boy and probably made his father angry by the things that he did.

Augustine did not love his father but he certainly loved his mother, Monica, very much. Monica was a Christian and belonged to a family that had been Christians for many years. So, as a child, she was taught to believe and to practise the Christian religion.

Patricius and Monica had another son, Navigius,* and a daughter named Perpetua,† but we do not know much about Augustine's brother and sister.

Augustine was not a Christian, although Monica had taught him many things about Christ and about the Christian faith. But Patricius did not want his small son to be baptized: Monica obeyed her husband's commands and Augustine was not made a member of the Christian Church. All the same, the child met many Christians. 'We saw that there were men who prayed to God and we asked them about this. They told us that, although we could not see God, he would hear us and help us. So I began to ask God to stop my teachers from beating me at school. But God did not stop them and my parents laughed at me, when I came home after a beating.'

When Augustine was a small boy, he became ill very suddenly one day. He had a violent pain in his stomach and a high fever. His mother was sure that he was going to

* Navi'gius   † Perpet'ua

die and, indeed, she planned that he should be baptized immediately. The boy himself, fearing that he was very near his death, agreed at once to the plan. Even Patricius seems to have agreed to the idea that his son should be made a Christian before he died.

But while Monica was preparing for her son's baptism, the boy's fever left him and he became well as suddenly as he had fallen sick. So then all the plans were changed and there was no baptism.

2

Augustine at School

━━●━━●●●●●●●●━━●━━

IN the school at Tagaste, Augustine learned to read and to write and to do arithmetic; all these lessons were in the Latin language, the language of Rome. When he wrote a book about his own life, Augustine said, 'I loved the Latin language. Not the Latin that I learned from my first masters, because they taught me only to read and to write and to do sums, and I hated that. But when I began to read Latin books and stories, then I loved Latin.'

Augustine and his school friends also had to learn the Greek language, for it was used in so many countries at that time. Years later, Augustine wrote: 'Even now I don't understand why I hated the Greek language so much, when I was a child and was taught it at school.' But Latin was the language that the boy heard in his own home and therefore he learnt it easily. He found that the difficulty of learning the strange Greek language was so great that he was always afraid of being punished by his teachers. Yet he liked the stories, which he read in the Greek books that he studied at school.

More than all his lessons Augustine loved to play ball with his friends. He spent a great deal of time in playing, when he ought to have been preparing his lessons. He was often beaten for this by his teachers.

He remained at the school in Tagaste until he was fourteen years old. He was a quite ordinary boy; he loved to have fun and often did all kinds of things that boys like to do. 'I often told lies to my teachers and to my parents', wrote Augustine in his book. 'Sometimes, too, I stole food from the storeroom of my parents' house or from the table at home. I did this because I wanted to eat food when it was not the time for a meal. Or sometimes because I wanted to have something to take to school for my friends. I gave them the food I had stolen and, in return, they gave me their games.'

Augustine was a great player of games. Like most small boys he loved to win, and was very sad if he lost a game. Sometimes he cheated in order to win. 'But', he wrote, 'if my friends found that I had cheated them, I was very angry and refused to admit what I had done.'

To his teachers, Augustine probably seemed to be a lazy boy, who could have done much better work if he had tried harder. He was not in any way stupid, but he avoided work whenever he could.

When Augustine was fourteen, he went to a bigger school in another town. This town was called Madaura and was about thirty miles from Tagaste. He went to that school in order to learn a study called Rhetoric. Rhetoric was the art of speaking or writing in such a way as to obtain the agreement of the hearer or the reader of the words. This art was followed by boys who wanted to study law, but it is possible that the masters at Tagaste did not include Rhetoric among the subjects that they taught. So Augustine went to Madaura, where he began to learn Rhetoric and other things.

After a year at Madaura, however, the fifteen-year-old Augustine had to return home. Patricius knew that his son was a clever boy, even if he were lazy. He decided that he would send the boy to the university at Carthage, but he needed a good deal of money to do that. Patricius could not afford to keep Augustine at Madaura and later to send him to Carthage. Since Augustine's parents both thought that Carthage was more important than Madaura, they decided to keep their son at home for a year and to save the money that he would need at Carthage.

So Augustine's school days were at an end for a time. The boy had not enough to do at home and he soon became very lazy. His parents and his friends all hoped that he would be a famous speaker and lawyer when he grew up, but they did not understand how to help Augustine in his boyhood.

No one thought that Augustine should find a wife, because everyone was thinking of the studies that he would follow at Carthage. Indeed, Monica told her son that he should be careful to avoid all girls and young women, so that he should not be tempted to do wrong or to marry. Yet the custom in North Africa was that boys should marry when they were fifteen or sixteen years old.

Both Patricius and Monica could think of little else but of the fact that their son would go to the university and then become a great and famous man. Monica feared that, if Augustine married, his wife would prevent him from working hard and becoming famous. But Augustine was becoming a young man and all his friends were young men too. It is true that he had one sister but he does not seem to have had any friends among the girls of Tagaste. When the other young men boasted about the girls that they knew,

Augustine sometimes told lies so that his friends should not laugh at him for not knowing any girls.

Because all the friends of Augustine were boys like himself, they used to play rough games together in the streets of Tagaste. When the days were over and the skies grew dark, these boys often stayed out in the streets and did not go home to bed until it was very late.

Sometimes they waited until darkness came and then went to a fruit tree, on which pears grew. This pear tree was near Patricius's garden and it had a great quantity of fruit on it; but the fruit was not very splendid and not always even ripe. But Augustine and his friends stole many pears from that tree. Having stolen the pears, the boys did not eat them; they threw them to the herds that were in the fields. The boys were not hungry. They stole the fruit simply in order to do something that they knew was wrong.

Afterwards, Augustine wrote about this fruit tree and the stolen pears. 'I should never have done it, if I had been alone. But when you belong to a group of young men and someone says, "Come on, let's go and do this or that", then you are ashamed to say "No".'

There were times when Augustine had plenty of fun with his friends at Tagaste; he knew that his father was poor but that he was making a great effort to send him to Carthage; he knew that Patricius was going to spend more money on his education than many richer men would spend on their sons. But, in spite of all this, the boy was not really happy at this time.

During the year that Augustine spent at home with his parents, Patricius decided that he himself would become a Christian. Perhaps he did it in order to please Monica. He does not seem to have tried to make his son ask for baptism too, so it is possible that he wanted to please his wife and that his own faith in Christ was not very strong. Patricius was not yet baptized but at this time he was a catechumen. A catechumen is someone who desires to be a Christian and who is preparing to be baptized.

But Augustine went to Carthage without having become a Christian.

3

Augustine and the Manichees

→•••●●•••←

CARTHAGE had been a famous and very beautiful city of North Africa for a long time. The distance round the walls of the city was probably as much as fifteen miles. But, at the end of the Second Punic War between Rome and Carthage in 201 B.C., the great city had been destroyed and the power of Carthage taken away.

After that, however, Rome built another city on the ruins of the old one and the new city also was very splendid. It was called 'the second wonder of the world' after the city of Rome itself. The Emperors of Rome built temples there for the false gods of the Roman Empire. They built theatres, where actors performed plays on the stage, showing stories of great men and women of ancient days. Among other famous buildings were baths, water springs and pipes for carrying water from one part of the city to another; besides all this there were many fine houses; burying places, coloured stone floors and walls; images of the false gods and of famous Roman Emperors and noblemen.

Carthage was a beautiful city, set on the coast of the Mediterranean Sea, with the forests and mountains of North Africa behind it.

To Augustine, the boy from Tagaste, this great city seemed very fine and full of interesting things. Especially he enjoyed the theatres and the plays which he saw acted there. Most of these plays told stories of great sadness, but Augustine shared the sorrow which the actors pretended to feel and, even with tears in his eyes, he was happy.

But most of Augustine's time was taken up with his study of Rhetoric. In his work as a student of the law, he did well: other students, and some of the university teachers too, began to speak of him as 'a great man in the Rhetoric School'. This praise pleased the young Augustine very much. He learned to speak very well and he looked forward to the time when he would be a famous lawyer.

By this time Augustine was nineteen years old. Patricius had died when his son was seventeen, but Augustine does not seem to have had much sorrow because of his father's death. In fact, he mentions the death of Patricius in his book only to explain why Monica herself had begun to pay for his education.

His teachers urged him to read a book called *Hortensius*,★ which had been written by the great Latin writer, whose name was Cicero. This book had a great effect on Augustine. In it he read of the search for wisdom and he began to understand that it was better to be wise than famous. He realized that what he spoke about was more important than the way in which he spoke about it.

Cicero was not a Christian and the name of Christ was not in the book at all. But Augustine still remembered the Christian teaching that Monica had given him when he was a boy. He knew that true wisdom belongs only to God. So

★ Horten'sius

he decided that he would begin to read the Bible. 'But I didn't think very much of the Bible at that time', wrote Augustine in his book. 'The language seemed to me to be much simpler than the beautiful language of Cicero. I think that I was too proud to understand the Bible and I soon gave up trying to do so.'

He gave up reading the Bible but he did not give up the search for wisdom and for truth. And so he met a company of men who were called Manichees and who had many strange beliefs. This false religion came from Persia in the third century and many believed it. The main thing that the Manichees believed was that good and evil were two equal kingdoms: God made the good kingdom and Satan made the evil one. For a long time, said the Manichees, these two kingdoms were quite separate. Then Satan attacked the kingdom of goodness; man was made by God so that he might defend the good kingdom, but man was defeated by Satan. After that, the two kingdoms were no longer separate. Good and evil became mixed together and both were in man. So, said the Manichees, when man did wrong it was not his fault. He could not help it, because evil was in him.

The important Manichees, who knew all the secrets of their religion, were called 'the elect' or chosen ones. They were not allowed to eat meat, to drink wine or to marry. But those who were ordinary members were allowed to live as they liked; only they had to serve the elect.

When he became a Christian, Augustine learnt that what the Manichees taught about the world could not be true, because the kingdom of good is the only real kingdom, which can have no end. But for several years Augustine did believe much of what the Manichees told him.

This made his mother very sad indeed. At first, she did not allow Augustine to enter his own home at Tagaste, when he came back from Carthage. However, one day she went to him and said, 'Augustine, my son, you may come back and live in my house and eat your food with me again.'

'What has happened to you, Mother?' asked Augustine. 'Why have you changed your mind about me?'

Then Monica replied, 'I have had a dream. In my dream I was very sad, because it seemed to me that you were destroyed by the false religion in which you believe. Then I seemed to be standing upon a piece of wood and I saw a splendid young man coming towards me, smiling happily. This young man asked me why I was so sad, and I told him that I was sad because you were destroyed. But the young man told me that you also were with me, where I was. Then I looked and saw you standing on the same piece of wood beside me.'

Augustine laughed and said, 'Perhaps your dream means that one day you will share the religion of the Manichees with me.' But Monica replied, 'No, it did not mean that; the young man told me that you were where I was; not that I should be where you are. It means that one day you, too, will be a Christian.'

Augustine was more interested in his mother's answer than in her dream and he thought a good deal about her words. All the same, he followed the teaching of the Manichees for nine years.

During all that time his mother continued to pray to God for her son. Once she went to a certain bishop and asked him to talk to Augustine and to teach him that the Manichees were wrong. The bishop refused to do this. 'Leave him alone,' he said. 'You must go on praying to God for him but he is not yet ready to be taught the truth. One day he will find out for himself, by his reading of books, that the teaching of the Manichees is false.'

Then the bishop added: 'When I was a young man, my mother taught me the religion of the Manichees. She made me read their books. She even made me copy some of them, so that I should really learn what was in them. Afterwards, I realized that the teaching of these books was not true, and I gave up the religion of those people. Your son will do the same.'

But Monica refused to accept what the bishop said. She still asked him again and again to see Augustine and to talk to him. At last, the bishop grew tired of her tears and of her cries and he said, 'Go away now. God bless you. It is quite impossible that your son should be destroyed after all these tears of yours.'

Then Monica believed that the words of the bishop were true and that they were really a promise from God, that Augustine should one day become a Christian.

4

The Search for Truth

————◀▸▰▰▰▰▸————

WHEN Augustine left Carthage, he began to teach Rhetoric at Tagaste. He lived with a woman, who was not married to him. She may have been a freed slave, who would not be allowed by Roman law to marry a man who had not been a slave. We do not know the reason that Augustine never married her, but we know that they lived happily together for many years. We know, too, that she was the mother of Augustine's son, Adeodatus.*

Now Augustine, who was still searching for truth, tried to find it in another study. This study was called Astrology, which means the study of the future by means of the position of the stars.

There was a very clever old man, named Vindicianus,† whom Augustine met at this time. In fact, Vindicianus was a doctor of medicine and also a man of authority under the Roman Government. This man met Augustine when he gave him a prize that Augustine had won by writing a poem. The old man and the young man became friends and used to talk together.

When Vindicianus knew that Augustine had begun to

* Adeoda'tus   † Vindicia'nus

study Astrology, he tried to stop him. 'When I was young,' said Vindicianus, 'I decided to follow the study of Astrology and to make that my profession. But I soon found that it is a false study and I began to learn medicine instead. You are a teacher of Rhetoric and you can earn your money by teaching. You do not need to study Astrology and you should not do so.'

'What you say may be true,' answered Augustine. 'But I know that very often the things that the astrologers say will happen, do happen. So there must be some truth in the study of Astrology.'

But the old man replied, 'That is not because Astrology is a true study, but because it happens by chance that sometimes the astrologers are right.'

However, Augustine would not listen to Vindicianus or even to his friend Nebridius,* who was young like himself. Nebridius laughed at the astrologers and tried to make his friend give up the study of their art. Augustine went on reading books about this study, though the words of Vindicianus made him begin to doubt the power of the astrologers.

On his return to his own town of Tagaste, Augustine met again a young man, who had been a school friend when they were both small boys. They had played together and had done their lessons together but they had not known each other very well. When they met again, as young men, they became great friends.

This young man was not a Christian but had been taught the Christian religion from his early days. Augustine led him to study the teaching of the Manichees and thus led him

* Nebri'dius

away from the truth. The two young men enjoyed their studies together and, for about a year, they spent a great deal of time in each other's company.

At the end of that year, Augustine's friend became seriously ill and remained so for a long time. His family were sure that he was going to die, because he lay, day after day, not knowing anything that was happening round him. Since death seemed so near, his family decided that the young man should be baptized. He was baptized, though he was still so ill that he did not know about it at the time. He seemed to be unable either to see or to hear the people who entered his room.

After his baptism, the young man became much stronger and his fever left him. Then Augustine was allowed to go and see his friend and to talk to him again. 'I hear that you have been baptized,' said Augustine, laughing. 'Do you suppose that that is why you are stronger now? You did not even know what was happening. What good can your baptism do to you?' And Augustine expected that his friend would join with him in laughing about his baptism.

To Augustine's great surprise, his friend replied: 'Do not ever let me hear you speak like that again. If you and I are to remain friends, you must never laugh at my baptism.'

Realizing that his friend was still very ill, Augustine decided to talk no more about the matter. But he thought that later, when his friend was quite well, he would do his best to make him laugh at his own baptism.

Such an opportunity never came. A few days after this, the young man's fever returned and he died. Augustine was not with him at the time of his death.

As soon as he heard of his friend's death, Augustine

became very sad. He hated all the things which once he had enjoyed with his friend; even his country and his home seemed different, because he knew that he would not see his friend again. At first, Augustine could hardly realize that his friend was dead; sometimes he almost expected to see him walking along the street. So great was Augustine's sorrow that he half wanted to die, and yet was afraid of death.

He could find no happiness in books or in music, in games, in good food or in the beautiful country round Tagaste. It seemed to him that all beauty had died with his friend. In fact, he could no longer bear to live in Tagaste, where he had been so happy before his friend's death, and he decided to return to Carthage and to teach Rhetoric there.

As time went on, Augustine made many new friends and began to be happy again. He also began to write and wrote two or three books, which he addressed to a famous Roman speaker, named Hierius.* Augustine had never met Hierius, but had often heard other men speak well of him, and knew that Hierius was the kind of man that he himself would have liked to be.

After Augustine had written those books, at the age of twenty-six or twenty-seven, he soon forgot them and, later, he could not even remember how he had lost his copy of them. But at the time the work employed his mind happily and helped him to forget his great sorrow.

While Augustine was teaching Rhetoric in Carthage, a famous Manichee, named Faustus,† came to that city. Augustine had wanted to meet Faustus for a long time, because he had heard that he was a very clever man and a

* Hier'ius   † Faus'tus

great speaker. Indeed, when he did hear Faustus speak in public, he realized that the man had a wonderful gift of speech. But already Augustine had begun to think that the teaching of the Manichees did not agree with what he himself knew by experience. And he read many other books, which taught quite different ideas. So, one day, he talked to Faustus and asked him many questions.

Then Augustine was very disappointed, because he saw that Faustus knew less than he knew himself. This was important, for from that time Augustine knew that he would never find the truth in the religion of the Manichees. He had gone to Faustus in order to be taught by him but very soon it was Augustine who was teaching Faustus. Augustine was Master of Rhetoric at Carthage and, having been asked by Faustus to do so, he began to give the Manichee private lessons.

However, the more Augustine knew about Faustus, the more he realized that he must look for truth somewhere else. But, as he could not find anything better at that time, he decided not to change his faith then.

5

Augustine in Rome

>••••••••••◄

AUGUSTINE was not very happy as a teacher at Carthage. Some of his fellow-teachers knew this and, one day, they said to him: 'Why don't you go to Rome and teach there? You could earn more money in Rome than you do here. You would also have more honour there, because Rome is the centre of the world. Only the best teachers are employed in Rome.'

Others said, 'If you went to Rome, you would find that the students behave much better there. Here you know that, sometimes, the students who are studying under other masters come to your classes. Because they are not your own students, they are rude and noisy, and they cause you much trouble. But in Rome the students are not allowed to go to the classes where their own masters are not teaching.'

Augustine certainly wanted money and honour, for he was eager to do well in his profession. But the idea of having quiet, hard-working students pleased him even more. When he himself had been a student in Carthage, he had never joined the noisy groups of young men, who enjoyed making trouble. As a teacher, however, he had to bear their foolishness, because custom did not allow him to punish them.

After a good deal of thought, Augustine made up his mind to leave Carthage and to go to Rome. He told Monica what he intended to do. 'Mother, I cannot continue to teach in Carthage, for I am much troubled by the students there. I shall take my wife and my son and I shall go to Rome.'

Monica was very sad when she heard this, and she did all she could to stop her son. She left Tagaste and travelled to Carthage immediately, to try to prevent Augustine from going. In fact, all her life, Monica tried to make her son do what she wanted him to do but this time she did not succeed. She was afraid that, at Rome, he would meet many false teachers and be driven farther and farther away from the Christian faith. Also she loved him very much and did not want to lose him. But it is possible that she was thinking more of what she wanted than of what was best for her son. 'My son,' she said, 'you will make me very unhappy if you go. If you leave Africa and travel across the sea, perhaps I shall never see you again. Please do not go. Stay here with me and let us be happy together, as we used to be.'

However, Augustine was determined to go and would not listen to his mother. Then she tried to make him take her too. 'If you must go, my son,' she said, 'then let me come with you and I will look after you in the city of Rome. It is not good for us to be in different lands; I cannot bear to remain here if you go to Rome.' But again Augustine refused to take her with him or to change his plans. And so the talk went on between them.

At last, Augustine decided that the only way to go was to pretend that he was not going and yet to leave Africa secretly. 'Mother, I have a great friend, who is going to Rome,' he told her. 'I must go to the harbour, where his ship is waiting for a good wind, so that they can sail to Italy. I cannot let him go, without saying good-bye to him.'

When Monica replied, 'I will not go back to Tagaste without you,' Augustine said: 'There is a little church near the harbour. I will take you there this evening and you can remain there while I see my friend.' So he took her to that place.

But, during that night, Augustine took his wife and son and secretly went on board the ship. Early in the morning, the wind blew and filled the sails of the ship. So they sailed away from Africa across the Mediterranean Sea.

Next morning, Monica learned what her son had done and how he had lied to her. She was very sad and returned alone to her home in Tagaste, while Augustine went on towards Rome.

Rome was a most wonderful city, the great capital city of the Roman Empire, the city of famous men and of wonderful buildings. Most young men from North Africa would have been delighted to have the chance to go to Rome. Once there, they would have admired all the splendid things they saw. In his book, however, Augustine wrote nothing about the greatness of Rome, about the wide streets and fine buildings that were all about him.

The reason seems to have been that he was not happy in Rome.

Almost as soon as he arrived in the city, Augustine fell ill with a serious fever; he believed that he would have died if his mother had not been praying for him.

The man, in whose house he lay ill, was a member of the Manichees and, when Augustine grew well again, he met many of the man's friends and some of them were among the elect Manichees. Together they discussed many ideas about life and the nature of the world, but they did not find truth and Augustine remained unsatisfied.

When he was quite well again, Augustine began his work as a teacher of Rhetoric at Rome. Gradually he collected some pupils, who came to him at the house where he was living in order that they might study under him. But it was not long before Augustine found that the students of Rome were not much better than those of Carthage.

It is true that they did not cause trouble in the same way but, when the time came for them to pay their masters, they suddenly disappeared and went to study under another teacher. Augustine was not rich and he had his wife and son to support, so he suffered from this behaviour of his pupils.

While he was in Rome, Augustine spent much time with his friend, Alipius.* Alipius had been born in Tagaste but was several years younger than Augustine. In fact, he had been one of Augustine's pupils, first at Tagaste and later at Carthage. His parents were important people in the town of Tagaste and were determined that their son should have a good education. After a time, Alipius left Carthage and went to Rome in order to study law there and he was already in Rome when Augustine arrived in the city.

Since Augustine was not happy in Rome, he began to look for an opportunity to go somewhere else and his opportunity soon came.

The people of the city of Milan asked the Prefect, or officer, of the city of Rome to send them a Master of Rhetoric. Milan was not such a famous city as Rome itself

* Alip'ius

25

but it was a splendid town and very important, because the Emperor and his mother lived there. The people of Milan asked Symmachus,* the Prefect of Rome, to choose a Master and to pay for his journey to Milan out of public money. When Augustine heard about this, he asked some of his friends among the Manichees to help him.

All the teachers of Rhetoric who wanted to go to Milan had to make a public speech in front of Symmachus, so that he might choose the best speaker. And it was Augustine who was chosen to go to Milan as Master of Rhetoric.

* Symma'chus

6

He meets Bishop Ambrose

➤➤•••••••◆••••◄

THE departure of Augustine for the city of Milan had great importance in his life, because it was his first real step towards becoming a Christian. One man, whom Augustine met in Milan, was the person whom God used to bring the young Master of Rhetoric to the Church. This man was Ambrose, Bishop of Milan.

Ambrose had been born in France about the year 340 and was the son of the Roman Prefect of that part of France, then called Gaul. He was sent to Rome to study law and, later, did well in his chosen profession at Milan. In the year 370, Ambrose was appointed Prefect of the provinces or districts of Liguria and Æmilia: he continued to live at Milan, which was the centre of government for these provinces.

When Auxentius,* Bishop of Milan, died in 374, there was a quarrel about who should be the next bishop. The quarrel was between the Christians who followed the true teaching, which was taught by the Apostles, and Christians who were called Arians, because they believed the false teaching of a man named Arius.† Arius had taught that

* Auxen'tius   † Ā'rius

3*

Christ was not truly God. He said that Christ had, at some time, been created by God and was therefore not equal with him. Auxentius had been an Arian and many people wanted another Arian bishop to follow him. Others wanted a 'Catholic', or true believer, to be the new bishop.

One day there was a great meeting in the market place, at which Ambrose spoke to the people. He was not a Christian himself at that time but a catechumen, preparing for baptism. However, he used his knowledge of law and of public speaking to try to make peace between the two parties in the Church. Everyone knew that Ambrose was a good man and they respected his judgement.

When Ambrose had finished speaking, an extraordinary thing happened. A young boy, who was standing at the back of the crowd, suddenly began to cry out: 'Ambrose for Bishop! Ambrose for Bishop!' The people all round him heard his words and they, too, began to call out: 'Ambrose for Bishop!' until the whole crowd was shouting those words.

Ambrose himself was surprised and not at all pleased. 'How can I be bishop?' he asked. 'I am not even baptized yet. What you say is quite impossible and very foolish.'

But everyone believed that the words of the young boy had been a message from heaven, and both parties, the Catholics and the Arians, agreed to have Ambrose, the lawyer, as their new bishop. Nothing that Ambrose could say or do made any difference. The people of Milan had made up their minds. They asked the Emperor, Valentinian I,* to command Ambrose to be Bishop and the Emperor did so.

* Valentin'ian

28

Accordingly, Ambrose was baptized and, eight days after his baptism he was made a priest and bishop of the Church. As Bishop of Milan, Ambrose soon became famous, because he was not afraid to speak the truth to the Emperor and he fought against all false teaching.

This was the man who was Bishop of Milan when Augustine came to that city as Master of Rhetoric.

Augustine soon went to hear Ambrose speak to the people and knew that he was listening to the words of a great man. For Ambrose pleased the young Master of Rhetoric by the way in which he spoke; and, still more, by the authority with which he spoke about the Christian faith.

Gradually Augustine came to realize that the words of Bishop Ambrose were true words and he decided to become a catechumen. So, although he was not yet a Christian, he gave up the teaching of the Manichees completely.

When Augustine had been in Milan about a year, his mother left Africa and came to Italy to join him. Later we learn that her other son, Navigius, was with her in Italy and so it is likely that he travelled with her at this time. As soon as Monica reached Milan, Augustine told her that he had given up the teaching of the Manichees and had become a catechumen. 'I am indeed glad to hear this,' answered Monica, 'and I hope that before I die I may see you become a faithful Christian.' Monica did not say any more about it to her son but she prayed to God a great deal. Also she often went to hear Bishop Ambrose speak; she admired him very much, because he had taught Augustine the truth.

Sometimes, when the people went to see Bishop Ambrose in his house, they found him reading. On such occasions, the Bishop did not even look up from his book to see who had come in; he simply continued to read. No one dared to speak to the Bishop when he was reading; so, after a time, his visitors stood up and went quietly away again. This custom of the Bishop's meant that Augustine had no opportunity to speak to him privately or to ask him the many questions that he longed to ask. For this reason Augustine had to be satisfied with the public words of Ambrose and with his own reading of books.

All this time Augustine remained Master of Rhetoric at Milan and he had a great deal of work to do. In the mornings he taught his students; later in the day his time was taken up with visiting important people, who could help him to become famous and honoured. He also spent much time in preparing and writing papers about the art of Rhetoric: he sold these papers to his students to help them with their studies and to gain more money for himself.

With so much to do, Augustine found it easy to decide that he had not much time in which to study the Christian faith.

7

*He talks with Simplicianus**

———•••••••••———

AUGUSTINE was not without friends in Milan. Alipius had not wanted to remain in Rome when his friend left and had therefore followed him to Milan, where he continued to study law. Another friend, who had come to Milan in order to be with Augustine, was Nebridius. Nebridius and Augustine had known each other in Carthage and it was he who had laughed at his friend's efforts to study Astrology. Augustine had not listened to him then. Now, however, he was glad to have his two friends with him in the great city where he was teaching.

Although Augustine was now thirty years old, it seemed to him that his life was not much different from the life he had lived as a nineteen-year-old student. He and his friends still met to read books and to discuss what they read, always hoping to find truth.

Yet, in his heart, Augustine already knew that he could find truth only in the Christian Church.

The delights of honour and of fame seemed very great to him. 'I have many important friends,' he said to himself. 'If I asked them to help me, I might even be appointed

* Simplicia'nus

Governor of some district. Perhaps I could find a rich wife, so that I should no longer be too poor and then I should have everything that I need.'

It was Alipius who urged Augustine not to marry. 'If you marry,' he said, 'we shall not be able to go on reading books together and searching for wisdom.' 'That is not true,' answered Augustine. 'There are many men who have married and who have continued to love their friends. Yes, and they have continued to search for wisdom.'

In the end it was Augustine who made his friend Alipius change his mind and both men began to think about marriage.

Monica urged Augustine to marry and she helped him to find a wife. The girl whom Monica chose for him was too young to be married; she was only a child. Augustine had to agree to wait two years until the girl would be old enough to marry him. But Monica would not hear of Augustine's marrying anyone else.

The parents of the girl, who was going to marry Augustine, were not happy about his first wife, who was still with him in Milan, although she had never been married to him. Monica talked to the girl's parents and they all agreed that Augustine must send the woman home to Africa. Augustine did not want to do this, but he knew that she would have to leave him before he married. So he obeyed his mother and sent the woman away. This made both of them very unhappy; what made the woman even more unhappy was that Augustine decided that their son, Adeodatus, must remain with him in Milan.

After she had gone, Augustine was so unhappy that he tried to forget his sadness by asking another woman to live with him as his wife, though she too was never married to him.

The fact was that Augustine tried to find happiness in many ways at this time, because he did not want to admit that he could not be happy any more outside the Church. One way in which he and his friends made plans for their happiness was that they decided that they would all go and live together in some quiet place, where there would be no other people. They thought that they would have time to read and study and that, if they shared all their money and their goods, they would not need to be rich. Each year, two of them would be chosen to look after the needs of the whole company. In that way, the others could live quietly, without working or meeting other people.

This plan seemed very good to Augustine and to all his friends. But some of his friends were married and he himself intended to marry when the girl was old enough. One day one of the men said, 'Do you think that our wives will like to live away from other people, with no money or goods of their own?' Then, one by one, the married men answered: 'No, I am sure that my wife will not agree to our plan at all.' 'My wife would be very angry, if I told her what we are going to do.' 'As for me, my wife is always asking me to give her more money; she would never agree to share what we have with anyone else.'

So the young men had to give up their idea of living as a company of people, sharing all their possessions and living away from other men. They continued, in fact, to live their ordinary lives among the other citizens of Milan. And Augustine continued to read many books in his search for wisdom and for truth.

As time went on, Augustine realized that he must have

help from a Christian. He knew that it would be difficult to find an opportunity to talk to Bishop Ambrose himself. But he remembered that a holy priest, named Simplicianus, lived in Milan. This good old man was the priest who had baptized Ambrose.

'Well,' thought Augustine, 'if I cannot talk to Bishop Ambrose, I can at least go and see Simplicianus.' And he set off to find the old man.

When Augustine came to the old priest's house, Simplicianus greeted him kindly and they sat down to talk. 'I have been reading many books and have searched for truth for many years,' Augustine told him. 'Some of the books which I have read were translated into Latin by Victorinus,★ who used to be Master of Rhetoric at Rome. I believe that Victorinus afterwards became a Christian.'

Then Simplicianus was very pleased to hear that Augustine had read those books. 'I knew Victorinus well when I was in Rome,' said the old priest. 'He was a very wise man, famous for his great knowledge. He had taught many of the great men of Rome, the men who ruled the city and the empire. In fact, Victorinus was so famous that an image of him had been set up in the city of Rome. That was a great honour; but afterwards he received an even greater honour, though quite a different one.'

Then Simplicianus continued: 'Victorinus read the Bible frequently and also the books of many Christian authors. Sometimes, when no one else could hear him, he said to me: "You know I am already a Christian." But always I gave him the same answer, that I would not believe him or think of him as a Christian until I saw him in the Church of Christ.

★ Victorī'nus

35

Victorinus used to laugh and say, "Do the walls of a church make a man a Christian?" The truth was that Victorinus was afraid to become a Christian publicly, because he thought that the rulers of Rome would then become his enemies.

'However, he continued to read the Bible and, one day, he said to me quite suddenly: "Simplicianus, let us go to the church; I have made up my mind to ask for baptism." Of course, I was very happy when I heard these words and I went with him. He began to be taught the Christian religion and to prepare for baptism. When the people of Rome heard about this, many of the rulers were very angry.'

Simplicianus was silent for a moment and then he went on: 'You know, Augustine, that it is the custom for men to say publicly that they believe in Christ, before they can be baptized. However, on this occasion, as Victorinus was so famous, the priests said that they would allow him to do this privately. But Victorinus refused to do it privately. He stood up in front of the citizens of Rome and told them honestly that for many years he had believed false things. And he told them that now he knew that the Christian religion was the only true religion. Then, having said publicly that he believed in Jesus Christ, he was baptized and, kneeling down, he received the sign of the cross of Christ upon his head.'

When Simplicianus had finished speaking, Augustine knew that he himself desired to have the courage to do what Victorinus had done.

8

The Visit of Pontitianus[*]

The Visit of Pontitianus[*]

In order to understand why Augustine waited so long before becoming a Christian and how, at last, the battle inside himself ended for him, it is necessary to realize how strongly he was held back by the desires of his body and of the world. We have already seen that Augustine loved a woman for many years; that when she had to leave him he did not want to wait for the young girl, whom he was to marry. He took another woman as his wife during the two years of waiting.

Augustine was afraid that, if he became a Christian, he would be called by God to be a priest and to live a single, unmarried life, He did not think that he could bear this.

Then, again, Augustine loved the fame and honour of the world. He wanted to be known and honoured by men; he wanted money and comfort. He was afraid that, if he became a Christian, he might lose all this.

Therefore, long after his mind had accepted the fact that truth is in Christ, his will held him back from the Christian Church. So the battle went on. Ambrose had helped him to choose; the prayers of Monica helped him and the words

[*] Pontitia'nus

of the old priest, Simplicianus, helped him. Still Augustine waited.

The next person who helped him was an African, named Pontitianus. One day, when Nebridius was out, Augustine and Alipius were sitting together. Pontitianus, who was an officer of the Emperor's house, came to see Augustine about some business. After they had discussed this business, the three men began to talk together about other matters.

There was a book lying on the table in front of Augustine; Pontitianus picked it up, thinking that it was a book of Rhetoric which Augustine used in his work. To his surprise, he found that it was a copy of the *Letters* of Saint Paul. 'I am glad to see that you have been reading this book,' he said to Augustine, 'and I am rather surprised. But, as you know, I am a Christian and so it pleases me to find this book in your house.'

Augustine answered, 'Although I am not a Christian, I often read the Bible.'

Then Pontitianus began to tell the two friends about Antony of Egypt, a famous Christian. This holy man lived in the desert of Egypt for almost the whole of his long life. He went away from the cities and villages in order to be quiet and to be alone with God. He spent his life in prayer. To his surprise, a great many men followed him to the desert and expressed their desire to live the same kind of life. Antony had to provide for his followers but arranged that each should live in a separate hut, and that they should meet only at times of special prayer.

Although the name of Antony of Egypt was well known among Christians, Augustine and Alipius had never heard of him.

After telling the friends about Antony and his 'hermits', or followers, who gave up their lives to prayer, Pontitianus told them that just outside Milan itself there was a house where such men lived. These men, however, were called monks instead of hermits, because they lived all together in one house. They were looked after by Bishop Ambrose himself, who often visited them. Yet neither Augustine nor Alipius knew that these men were there. Both of them were so much interested in what Pontitianus was telling them, that they remained silent and allowed their African visitor to go on talking.

'Once I was in the city of Trèves, where the Emperor was attending some games. While we were waiting for him, I went for a walk with three companions. After a time, I walked on with one of these three men and the other two walked together. As these other two wandered up and down, they came to a small house, where some Christians lived. In this house they found a book about Antony of Egypt and one of the men began to read it. As he read, he began to desire to do as Antony had done.

'These men were both servants of the Emperor, as I was. Suddenly the man who was reading the book said to his friend: "What are you and I really working for? What can we hope to get as a reward for all our work? And can we have any higher reward than to be called the friends of the Emperor? But there is always danger in being the friend of a great ruler on earth. And, in order to become the Emperor's friends, we should have to work hard for many years. But, if I desire it, I can at this very moment become the friend of God."

'He continued to read and then he said, "Now I have made

up my mind and I am going to leave the service of the Emperor and give my life to God." His friend agreed to go with him.

'Soon afterwards, my other friend and I joined these two men and suggested that they should return with us, because by that time it was nearly evening. However, they told us that they had decided not to return with us. Instead, they were going to remain with the other Christians in the small house, and give themselves to God. So my friend and I returned alone to the Emperor and left these two men in the small house.'

Then Augustine knew that the time had come when he must become a Christian too. He realized at last that he had not been waiting to find the truth but waiting for the courage to follow the truth, which had been shown to him by the Christians.

After Pontitianus had finished speaking, Augustine turned to Alipius and said, 'This story is terrible. Men like these two men, who have had no education, can find the courage to leave everything for God. You and I, with all our learning, are still afraid to do so. Are we ashamed to follow, because they have had the courage before we have? Shall we not be much more ashamed, if we do not even try to follow them?'

He had come to the most important day of his whole life.

9

'Take up and read'

→•◦◦◦●◦◦◦•←

PONTITIANUS had gone.

Augustine had reached the moment when he had to choose, once and for all. Suddenly it seemed to him that the house was too small; he must be outside in the air. Leaving Alipius behind, he rushed out into the garden, knowing that whatever happened in the next hour would be very important.

Alipius ran out after him, realizing that his friend had come to a point, from which he could not turn back, and not wishing to leave him alone in his trouble.

Together they sat down as far from the house as they could. Augustine said no word. But he tore at his hair, struck himself upon the head, twisted his fingers in and out of one another, and showed Alipius clearly the great battle that was in his heart.

No word was spoken, yet Augustine knew why he had failed. In his heart he almost heard the words: 'You are trusting in your own strength and that is why you have no strength at all. Trust only in God, for he will not leave you or allow you to fail.'

There are some moments in the life of every man which

cannot be shared, even with a dear friend. With tears running down his face, Augustine stood up and went away from Alipius. Far enough away to be really alone. Alone with God.

This time, Alipius understood that he must not follow Augustine and he remained where he was. Augustine threw himself down under a tree and cried aloud to his God: 'How long, O Lord, how long? How long will you be angry with me? O do not remember the wrong that I have done.'

Listen! What is that? Somewhere a voice singing. Like a boy or girl singing in a house not far off. 'Take up and read. Take up and read.' What strange words. What can they mean?

Augustine could remember no game the children played which had a song with words like that.

Suddenly he understood.

The words were words from heaven, urging him to open the book of Saint Paul's *Letters* and to read whatever was written on the page at which he might open it.

Then Augustine remembered that Antony of Egypt had read the Gospel once, it seemed by chance, and had read the words of Christ as though they had been particularly said to him. 'Go, sell all that you have, and give to the poor, and you shall have treasure in heaven. And come, follow me.' Those had been words which had changed the whole course of Antony's life.

Quickly, Augustine ran back to the place where Alipius was sitting. He had left the book of the *Letters* of Saint Paul lying there when he got up.

He picked it up, opened it and silently read from the first

words that his eye saw: 'Not with the making of trouble or the drinking of too much wine; not with women or with the wild desires of the body; not with quarrelling or envying but put on the Lord Jesus Christ and do not provide for the flesh, to satisfy its evil desires.'

Augustine read no more. There was no need to read any more. For those words, and those words alone, were like a clear light in his mind, putting away all doubt.

Quite calmly, Augustine shut the book, marking the place where he had read by putting his finger or some other mark between the pages; then he told his friend Alipius all that had happened. In his turn, Alipius told Augustine all that he himself had been thinking, while Augustine had been under the tree. 'Show me what words you read in Saint Paul's *Letters*,' said Alipius.

Augustine showed him the passage and, taking the book in his hands, Alipius read on beyond the words that Augustine had read. These were the words that Alipius read: 'Receive him that is weak in the faith.'

Then he said to Augustine, 'I am weak in the faith; therefore those words mean that you are to take me with you and that we are to become Christians together.'

Without any further delay, Augustine and Alipius went back to the house to find Monica; for they knew that she must be the first to hear their good news. As soon as they found her, Augustine told her that he and Alipius were going to ask for baptism. Then he told her everything that had happened in the garden.

Thus the words of the old bishop had come true: 'It is quite impossible that your son should be destroyed, after all these tears of yours.' Monica remembered how the old man had spoken these words to her many years before, and she thanked God. She thanked God for saving Augustine from false religions and for having turned him so strongly away from his former life. Indeed, Augustine no longer desired a wife or the fame and honour of this world.

'You also were with me where I was,' Monica had said many years before, when she had told her dream to her son. Now truly she could say, 'Augustine, my dear son, you are where I am.' And her joy was full.

At that time it was the custom of the Church that catechumens should be baptized on the night between Holy Saturday and Easter Sunday. Therefore Augustine and Alipius could not be baptized immediately. But there was to be no more empty waiting for Augustine. He began at once to make plans to change his way of life.

He decided to stop teaching Rhetoric. However, as yet he and Alipius told no one that they were going to become Christians, except Monica and a few close friends. So Augustine made up his mind that he would continue to teach until the end of that term. The term ended when the time of the harvest came and there were not more than three weeks of the term remaining. He decided not to leave his post as Master of Rhetoric until then, because at that time he did not wish to discuss his affairs publicly.

He knew that many parents would try to force him to continue with his teaching work, so that their sons might be taught by him. As it happened, however, Augustine was helped by an illness that came to him. He had been working very hard and speaking in public very often. Moreover, he had had an extremely unusual experience in his most secret life. He was very tired and his voice began to fail him, with a sickness of the throat. Even if he had wished to continue teaching, he could no longer have done so.

But, speaking with difficulty and in a very quiet voice, he managed to teach until the end of that term.

It was then that a friend, named Verecundus,* showed great kindness to Augustine and Alipius. Verecundus was not yet a Christian and did not then intend to become one. He was sad that his two friends were going to be baptized, because he realized that they would leave his company. But he offered his country house to his friends, so that they could leave Milan and live quietly at Cassiciacum,† where his house was.

At last the day came when Augustine was free. As he went to Cassiciacum with Monica, Alipius and his son, Adeodatus, he was very happy. At Cassiciacum, Augustine spent much of his time in writing. He wrote, among other things, many letters to his friend, Nebridius and, of course, he read the Bible very often.

When the time of harvest and of wine-making was over, before the next term began, Augustine informed the citizens of Milan that he did not wish to continue as Master of Rhetoric. 'You must find another man who will teach your students. I have made up my mind to serve God only; and, indeed, I cannot teach, because it is difficult and painful for me to breathe, because of this sickness in my throat.'

At the same time, Augustine wrote a letter to Bishop Ambrose, telling him that he had long been a follower of the Manichees but had now determined to ask for baptism. He asked the Bishop to suggest some books for him to read.

* Verecun'dus   † Cassicia'cum

Difficult study

The Bishop replied that he should study the book of Isaiah, that great man of God. Augustine began to do so, but found the book hard to understand. Accordingly, he laid it by, until he should understand more about the Christian faith.

10

The Death of Monica

WHEN the time came for Augustine to give in his name, as one who wished to be baptized at Easter, he and his family and friend returned to Milan. Alipius had decided to ask for baptism at the same time as Augustine and with them the boy, Adeodatus, was also to become a Christian. Adeodatus was fifteen years old and a very clever boy, who already showed signs of being able to understand many things which older men found too difficult for them.

So Easter came and Bishop Ambrose himself baptized Augustine, together with his son, Adeodatus, and his great friend, Alipius. It was the year 387; Augustine was thirty-three.

After his baptism, Augustine decided that they should all return to Africa. Now that he was no longer a teacher of Rhetoric, he had no affairs to keep him in Milan. Monica was no longer a young woman and it was natural for her to wish to go back to her own land.

They began their journey and reached Ostia, the harbour town at the mouth of the River Tiber, the river of Rome. At Ostia, they had to wait for a ship that was going to Carthage and, while they were waiting, they stayed in the little town.

One day Augustine and Monica were alone, sitting in the house at Ostia, beside a window from which they could see the garden of the house. Mother and son talked together, neither knowing that this was to be their last long conversation with each other.

They talked of God and of his great works. Then they became silent, each thinking of the wonderful goodness and love of God. At last Monica said, 'My son, there is nothing more that I desire in this world. I do not know whether there is anything more for me to do here or why I am still here. My great desire has always been that I should see you baptized before I died. Now I have seen this and more than this, for I see that God has made you his true servant and that you no longer desire the fame and honour of this world.'

About five days after this conversation, Monica became ill with a fever. One day she was so ill that she seemed not to know anything that was happening. Augustine and Navigius, who was also there, ran to her. Soon Monica was a little better and able to speak again. 'Where was I?' she asked her sons, but they could give her no answer. Then she said to them, 'I shall die and you must bury me here at Ostia.'

Augustine did not reply but Navigius said at once: 'No, Mother, do not speak of dying. Soon you will be better and we shall take you home to Africa.' But Monica knew that this would not happen.

A short time afterwards, she said again to both her sons: 'Bury my body where you will. That is not important. But I ask you that, wherever you are, you shall remember me before the altar of the Lord.' Then she remained silent, her sickness being too great for any more words.

Augustine was very happy when he heard his mother's words. He knew that she had hoped to go back to Africa before she died. She had even bought a piece of land, next to the place where Patricius was buried, in order that her body might lie beside his. But now she had learnt that the place where a Christian body is buried does not really matter very much. 'No place is far from God,' she had said to a woman at Ostia not many days before. 'He will know from what place to raise me again at the day of judgement.'

So, after nine days of illness, Monica died at the age of fifty-five.

Augustine quietly closed his dead mother's eyes. Suddenly the boy, Adeodatus, began to cry aloud. His own mother had gone back to Africa and now his grandmother was dead, and he was very sad. But Augustine and Navigius told the boy that Monica had died happily and in the true faith and that therefore he should be silent.

Then Evodius,* another Christian friend of Augustine's, began to read from the Bible and the others joined with him. Soon the news of Monica's death spread to other houses near and many Christian men and women came along to help Augustine. He was very sad, for his mother had died suddenly and he loved her very much, But he would not allow anyone to make a great noise of sorrow when they buried Monica; so they went to the burying place and returned from it without tears.

The book, which tells us all about the early part of Augustine's life is his own book, which he called his *Confessions*. He did not write this book until about the year 400. The main purpose of the book was to show three things.

* Evō'dius

First, that the only way of life for a Christian is to live within the Church, as a full member of it. Secondly, that the Church's teaching is true and can therefore satisfy every human need. Thirdly, the book is like a map of Augustine's own search for truth, and can therefore help other people to make the same journey, from false teaching to the truth.

But in his *Confessions* Augustine does not tell us anything about his life after Monica's death. So now we have to find out what happened from other records of history and from other books written by Augustine himself.

Augustine and Monica had planned to go to Africa, as we know, and were waiting at Ostia for a ship when Monica died. It seems that Augustine did not go to Africa that year after all. Instead, he went to Rome again, where he wrote several papers against the false teaching of the Manichees.

Perhaps he felt that he could not happily return alone to Tagaste so soon after his mother's death. Perhaps it was the new Bishop of Rome, Pope Siricius,* who asked him to return to Rome. Pope Siricius was a great enemy of the Manichees and may have wanted to use Augustine's experience of their teaching in his battle against them.

Whatever the reason for Augustine's staying in Italy may have been, it seems that he did not return to Africa until August of the following year, 388. In those days, when ships were driven only by sail, people did not travel by sea in the winter very much and so Augustine had to travel during the summer months.

When he returned to Tagaste at last, he returned alone. His son, Adeodatus, died not many months after the death of

* Siri'cius

Monica. On his return, the first thing that Augustine did was to sell his father's land and house and to arrange all the affairs of his dead parents.

Then with the money that he gained from the sale of the land, he opened a small house where Christian men could live together as monks. They lived very simply and spent much of their time in praying to God. For three years Augustine lived quietly with them, writing and studying the Christian faith.

11

Bishop of Hippo

————•••••••••••←

In the year 391, an important officer of the government said that he thought he could give up the honour and fame of the world in order to serve God, if he were able to talk to Augustine. This officer lived at a North African town called Hippo. Hippo was a town on the Mediterranean coast, built on the edge of a lovely little bay of clear blue water. Behind the town were rich and fertile plains, where the Numidians grew fruit and corn. Hippo was built on the banks of a river, which flowed to the Mediterranean from the mountains south of the town.

Augustine heard that the officer had declared a wish to see him and talk to him. He decided to go to Hippo to see the man.

The story of the way in which Ambrose had been chosen to be Bishop of Milan shows that, in those days, men were sometimes forced to become priests and bishops against their will. Augustine knew that the time might come when the Church would not allow him to remain quietly at Tagaste any more. But he was not afraid to go to Hippo, for Hippo already had a Bishop.

Valerius,* Bishop of Hippo, was a Greek. He could not

* Valēr'ius

understand the Punic language of North Africa and he did not know very much Latin. This made it difficult for him to rule over and care for the people in his charge. Moreover, he was an old man and the people of Hippo wanted a younger man as their bishop.

When Augustine appeared in the little town of Hippo, the crowd seized him and urged Valerius to make him a priest. Augustine did not want this at all. He wanted to be allowed to remain in peace at Tagaste, but he was not able to do so.

Augustine became a priest and was soon given the work of speaking to the people in Latin, a work that Bishop Valerius could not do. After a time, the younger man became the chief helper of the Bishop. Indeed, Valerius found Augustine so useful that he asked the chief Bishop to let Hippo have two bishops, himself and Augustine. Accordingly, Augustine was made Assistant Bishop of Hippo in 395 and, in the following year, he became Bishop of Hippo and remained in charge of the Church there until his death in 430.

He lived in Hippo as he had lived at Tagaste, in a house of monks. He continued to study and to write but often, of course, he had to leave his private work to do his work as Bishop of Hippo.

Besides his ordinary work as a bishop, Augustine was closely concerned with the Church's fight against false teaching. Almost immediately after he became a priest in 391, he began to work against an extremely powerful group called the Donatists. At that time there were probably more Donatists than Catholics in North Africa, and this group had nearly succeeded in dividing the whole African Church into two parts. That they did not entirely succeed in doing so was mainly due to Augustine.

But, in order to understand what the trouble was about, it is necessary to know something of the earlier history of the Donatist group.

It had all begun nearly 100 years before, when a man named Mensurius★ was made Bishop of Carthage. Many people said that he had given some of the holy books of the Church to the government soldiers when the Emperor had attacked the Christians. Accordingly they said that such a man could not be a bishop. Mensurius replied to his attackers that he had given the soldiers books of false teaching, which did not really belong to the Church. There were, however, other reasons for the hatred of the people towards him. Caecilian,† a priest at Carthage, was even more hated than Mensurius and when he was chosen as bishop, on the death of Mensurius, the people's anger was great indeed.

Some bishops, who were on the side of Caecilian, travelled quickly to Carthage in order to make him a bishop, and they did not wait for the bishops of the Province of Numidia to arrive. This made the trouble much worse. Bishop Felix of Aptunga was the chief bishop who consecrated Caecilian, thus making him a bishop. People then said that Bishop Felix, too, was a man who had handed Church property to the government.

A rich woman, who hated Caecilian because he had publicly found fault with her, now urged his enemies to act. A meeting of seventy bishops was held and, as a result of this meeting, two things happened. First, the bishops

★ Mensu'rius   † Caecil'ian

declared that Caecilian was not really a bishop because, they said, Felix could not consecrate him. Secondly, they chose a priest named Majorinus* and made him a rival Bishop of Carthage.

In this way, the two groups, the Catholics and the Donatists, as the party of Majorinus came to be called, were set up in Africa.

In the year 313, the Emperor Constantine agreed to stop the attacks against the Christian Church and to protect all Christians. He refused, however, to protect the followers of Majorinus. These followers then asked the Emperor to call a meeting of bishops from France, who were not directly concerned in the quarrel. Constantine did so, but the three bishops, who met in Rome together with many Italian bishops, all agreed that Caecilian was the true bishop of Carthage.

Still unsatisfied, the Donatists tried once again to get the Emperor on their side. But this time Constantine became angry with them and took their churches away from them, sending the Donatist leaders out of the country where they lived. About 320 he allowed them to come back again, but in that year the real argument lost its power, when it was learned that some of the leading Donatists had themselves given away Church property.

However, that was by no means the end of Donatism. What had begun as a religious movement gradually became something else. It became a fight between the poor of North Africa against those who were richer and possessed land. In this way it divided the members of one country against each other. Moreover, it was also a fight between the

* Majori'nus

Africans on the one hand and the power of Rome on the other. Thus it tried to divide the Church on a matter of race and showed signs of becoming a strong national movement.

The Donatists had failed to get what they wanted in a peaceful way. So they tried to get it by violence. Groups of men, who wandered round the North African villages, soon frightened all the Catholics and all who desired peace. These wandering men carried heavy sticks in their hands and were prepared to use them on anyone who did not agree with them. Men, women and children ran away in fear when they heard the cry of the Donatists, 'Praise to God!' shouted near their homes.

By the time that Augustine came to Hippo, the old question of whether Felix had been able to consecrate Caecilian was no longer important. But the real argument was about matters that deeply affected the whole Church.

Augustine was quick to see that the quarrel was really about two main points. If a bishop or priest were an evil man, could he bring the power of God to Christians in his work as a minister of the Church? Can people who do evil be members of the Church as well as good people?

These questions were very important, because they are about the whole purpose of the work of the Church and about the true nature of the Church itself.

Augustine realized the importance of these questions and he wrote an answer, putting forward the true teaching of the Church against the false teaching of the Donatists.

He said that the power which is given to man through the ministers of the Church does not come *from* those ministers but *through* them. The power comes from God and is entirely good. Therefore, the power remains good, even if the minister is not a good man.

Secondly, he said that the Church is holy, not because all its members are holy but because it is a society formed by God for holy purposes. In the Church there will always be good people and people who are not good: the Church is for all men and the purpose of the Church is to help all men to become better. Because the Church is God's society, it can never fail; and evil, outside it or inside it, can never overcome it.

12

The Teaching of Pelagius*

———•◆◆◆●◆◆◆◆•———

ANOTHER kind of false teaching with which Augustine was concerned was the teaching of a man from Britain, whose name was Pelagius.

Pelagius was a Christian monk, who went to Rome about the year 400. In Rome, where he had expected to find that the Christian religion was very strong and that its followers were good men, he found a very different state of affairs. Many Christians seemed to be living lives which were not according to the teaching of Christ. They thought a great deal about money and comfort and some of them were openly doing evil things. There were many others, who had given up the practice of their religion and who seemed to be making no effort at all to obey the commands of Christ and the rules of the Church.

While Pelagius was in Rome, he read Augustine's *Confessions*. In this book he found a sentence, which troubled him very much. The words were addressed to God: 'Give what you command and command what you will.'

Pelagius decided that these words meant that, unless God gave a man the power to obey, a man could not obey and need not even try to do so. 'This means,' he said 'that God

* Pelag'ius

alone decides whether a man is to be good. A man can do nothing about it by himself. I do not agree with this teaching. Even if we are bad, we can make ourselves good if we try hard enough.'

So Pelagius began to try to urge the people of Rome to make more effort to be good. He told them that they needed no special help from God, but that the ordinary power which every man receives from God was enough for them. Everything, he said, depended upon a man's own will. If a man wanted to follow the teaching of Christ and to obey his commands, then he could do so by his own effort.

The teaching of Pelagius was false, because he taught that man could save himself by his own strength. If this were true, it would really mean that it was not necessary for Christ to come to this world and to suffer and die in order to save men from evil.

At first, no one took very much notice of what Pelagius was teaching. In Hippo, Augustine was very busy in his fight against the Donatists, and it may even have been some time before he heard anything about the words of Pelagius in Rome.

Later on, however, when the city of Rome was attacked and taken in 410, many Romans escaped to Africa. Among them was Pelagius himself, who came to the city of Carthage. Perhaps he hoped that more people would listen to him there than in Rome. Certainly, he began to teach even more strongly than before that man needs no special help from God in order to save himself.

With Pelagius in Carthage was another man from Britain. Celestius* had studied law for many years but had

* Celes'tius

become a monk; when he arrived in Carthage, he asked whether he could become a priest. The Church, however, refused to allow this, because Celestius was a follower of Pelagius, and taught even more extraordinary things about the effects of evil and what a man must do to be saved.

When these two British monks came to North Africa, Augustine heard all about their teaching. He was determined to write an answer to the Pelagian teaching, as he had written against the Donatists with such success.

In fact, Augustine wrote several answers to this false teaching. The idea of the help given by God was a matter which was most important to Augustine. He could never forget the words which he had heard in the garden at Milan so many years before: 'You are trusting in your own strength and that is why you have no strength at all.'

The Bishop of Hippo knew very well that, if he had not received special help from God, he might still have been a Manichee or a slave to the desires of his own body. He did not believe that the will of man could be really free to choose good, unless God gave special help. So Augustine taught that a man could not be saved unless God gave him two kinds of help. First of all, special help even to want to be good and, after that, help to enable him to overcome his temptations and to go on trying to follow Christ.

The general opinion of the leaders of the Church was divided between the teaching of the British monk and that of the African Bishop. But this uncertainty did not last for long.

In 416 two great meetings of Church leaders in Africa agreed that Pelagius and his followers were wrong. The Pope himself gave judgement against Pelagius just before his own death. The next Pope, however, was Zosimus,* a Greek, who did not seem to be sure which was the true teaching. Celestius asked him to consider the judgement again but Pope Zosimus refused to pronounce either for or against Pelagius. While the Pope was waiting to see what would happen next, the Emperor decided that the spread of the Pelagian teaching must be stopped. Supported by the Emperor, the Pope found it easier to make up his own mind and agreed that Augustine was right.

Some of the Italian bishops were not so sure that Pelagius's teaching was wrong. They thought that the Pope's punishment of him was too severe and they refused to sign the judgement paper. It was well, perhaps, that two years later Pelagius himself died. The Church officially condemned his teaching at the Council of Ephesus in 431.

Not all Augustine's writings were written against false teaching. One of his most interesting books was called *Concerning the Work of Monks.* We know that, when Augustine was in Milan, he heard about the life of Antony of Egypt and about the monks who were living outside the city of Milan under the care of Bishop Ambrose. The life lived by those monks had a great influence on Augustine, in leading him towards the Church, and on his life afterwards.

Even before Augustine became Bishop of Hippo, he lived at Tagaste in a house of monks. After moving to Hippo he continued to live in this way. This is important, because Augustine was the first man to introduce this kind of Christian life into North Africa. For the life of Augustine's monks was very different from the life of the followers of

* Zosi'mus

Antony of Egypt. Antony's followers were called hermits, men who lived in separate huts in the desert. Augustine's monks, on the other hand, lived in one house together. Their life was lived in common and they shared all that they had.

Another very important difference was that the hermits spent their time in prayer, they did not work with their hands. But Augustine taught his monks that they ought to work in order to earn their food and other needs; his monks were clerks, who worked among the Christians at Hippo.

Concerning the Work of Monks was written about the problem of those monks who refused to work and who believed that they had a right to beg their food from other Christians.

13

'The City of God'

WE have seen that a great deal of Augustine's time was taken up with his fight against false teaching. But meanwhile much was happening in the world at that time and it was the events of history that urged the Bishop to write one of his greatest books.

The Goths were a powerful tribe of people who lived near the River Danube, and for many years they had been attacking the Roman Empire. In the time of Augustine, Alaric was the Gothic general and, in 402, he led his army to attack Northern Italy. A great battle was fought in that year between the Goths under Alaric and the Roman army, under a German general, named Stilicho.* Stilicho was a wonderful soldier and he won this battle, driving the Goths out of Italy again.

Four years later another tribe, the Vandals, crossed the great chain of mountains that guards the Northern part of Italy and marched to Florence. Here they were met by Stilicho, who drove them back also. These tribes had good reason to fear the strength and skill of this general. But in 408 Stilicho was killed.

When Alaric heard the news of his enemy's death, he

* Stili'cho

decided to try to attack Rome again. He managed to reach the city this time and, after many battles, captured it in 410.

The Goths were Christians and they were not nearly so cruel as many other tribes might have been. In fact, although many Romans escaped from the city and went to North Africa for protection, the people who remained in Rome were not treated too badly.

But the effect of the capture of Rome on the rest of the world was very great. One famous Christian writer expressed what many people were thinking, when he wrote: 'The whole world has been destroyed in one city.'

It was not until 413 that Augustine began to write his great work, *The City of God*. This book was really twenty-two books and it took Augustine thirteen years to complete it. He wrote it, because many people, who were not Christians, blamed the Christian Church for the trouble which had come to the city of Rome. They said that the old gods of the Romans were angry, because so many men and women had turned away from worshipping them in order to follow Christ. Because of this, they said, the true gods of Rome had refused to protect the city any more and the enemy had been able to conquer it.

In his book, the Bishop of Hippo showed that, when the Goths conquered Rome, many of those who believed in the old gods had, in fact, run to the Christian churches to beg for shelter there. No one had asked for protection in vain. So it seemed as though even those who were not Christians believed that more protection could be given by the Church than by the old gods.

But this was not the really important part of Augustine's book. He called the book *The City of God* because in it he described two cities: the city of the Christian Church and the city of the world. Those who live according to the will of God, for love of God, are citizens of the city of God; this city can never fail, and will bring victory and peace to its citizens.

The city of the world will fail and come to an end, because its citizens live to please themselves and do not obey God. Like the pride of Rome, the pride of the city of the world could lead only to ruin.

Perhaps the most important effect of the book was that Augustine thus showed that the Church is more important than the State. Hundreds of years after the death of Augustine, the Popes of Rome were able to make the power of the Church greater than the power of the government because of the influence of *The City of God*.

In this and in many other ways, the influence of Augustine remained long after he himself had died. Augustine lived at a time when the culture of the old world of the East was dying. By culture we mean the learning and thought of nations, often expressed in art, in music, in books and even in the customs of the people. The old culture was not a Christian culture, but no new one had come to take its place.

In fact, the real Christian culture of the West did not fully develop for about 800 years after Augustine, but it was he who did more to shape it than anyone else.

He himself knew the old culture well; he took from it all that was good and, by his own teaching, changed it, gave it new life, and made it the seed of the Christian culture of the later centuries, which are called the middle ages: that is, about the eleventh to the fifteenth century in European history.

It is interesting now, in the twentieth century, to remember that a great part of later European culture came
from an African seed.

Augustine was growing old and North Africa was no
longer at peace. After the Goths came the Vandals, a much
fiercer and more cruel tribe. Although they had once been
driven from Italy by Stilicho, they continued to make war.
They attacked Spain and then travelled on to North Africa.
They did much harm there and, in 430, they attacked the
town of Hippo.

All round the little town were the armies of the Vandals;
inside Hippo, the people tried hard to keep the enemy out.
But Augustine took no part in all this. The seventy-six-year-
old Bishop lay dying in his simple house.

'Write on the wall the Psalms of David,' said the Bishop.
'Let me see those great songs, that David wrote in sorrow
for his sin. Let me remember that I, too, have been a great
sinner.'

So Augustine died. Outside, there was the sound of battle.
But Augustine did not hear it.

That great African had come face to face with Truth at
last.

Index

Index